Whole

Sistaz Sharing Stories of Healing and Transformation

Compiled by
Angela J Barnes

If you purchase this book without a cover you should be aware that this book may have been stolen property and reported as "unsold and destroyed" to the publisher. In such case neither the author nor the publisher has received any payment for this "stripped book."

Copyright ©2015 B Life Publishing

All Rights reserved.

No part of this book may be reproduced or transmitted in any form or by any means without written permission from the author.

ISBN 10 – 069237082X
ISBN 13 - 9780692370827

Whole
Sistaz Sharing Stories of
Healing and Transformation

Cover Design: Hot Book Covers
(www.hotbookcovers.com)

DEDICATION

"Sometimes the strongest women are the ones who love beyond all faults, cry behind closed doors and fight battles that nobody knows about" - *Unknown*

To all the women in the world who had a story to tell and not a voice to speak.

Forward

In all my years on this earth I endured a lot of hurt and pain. All of us have. I misinterpreted the downs that I experienced as making my life worse. At that time, disappointments, hardships, obstacles were all happening to me just to make my life difficult and unfair. "God, must really hate me" is what I use to think. For a long time I threw myself a pity party with each dilemma I faced. I would allow the ramifications of "life" to get me down which would cause sadness, anger, and ultimately create a spirit of defeat. My pain would hold me hostage by replaying in my head everyone and everything in my life which I deemed as being against me. Once I allowed myself to get into that state of mind, it became arduous to see pass my most recent pain. I would wallow in it asking all my "whys." One day I reflected on all of my hardships and wondered "why." This time it wasn't in a complaining "I'm so fed up" tone, but it was a tone that was serious and curious as to how to make this very intricate thing called life work for me and not against me. Once I took that approach, I noticed that my life wasn't so bad after all. More importantly, I learned from studying myself and Kemetic culture that I could make those situations work in my favor regardless of how bad it initially seemed. As I continued to heal and transform my thinking, I realized that not only can my past and whatever I experience from that point forward work for me, but I could also use it to teach and assist others.

Angela Barnes' idea of WHOLE: Sistaz Sharing Stories of Healing and Transformation is excellent and needed. This book provides woman of Afrikan decent with a platform to share their stories which (1) allows these sistaz to sit and reflect without anger or resentment which facilitates further growth (2) illustrates how our adversities are not against us, but are meant to empower and enlighten us (3) allows those who currently cannot see past their problems to know that there's power in perception. If we perceive our problems as being against us, then that's what they will be and no one can tell us differently. If we perceive our downfalls, heartache, and troubles as stepping stones helping us to arrive at the next point in our life, then we wouldn't dread them. We would be thankful for them, because without them we wouldn't be the women we are now and continue to become. It's great to know that the women within this book were able to heal and transform themselves from the different things they have endured in life. Too many times we walk around broken. Too many times we walk around angry for no apparent reason. Too many times we ruin our plutonic and intimate relationships because of our extra baggage and misconceptions from all of the nonsense in our heads. When we say "enough is enough" then and only then is when things start to change for us. When we say "I want to heal" and put forth the effort to do so that is when things change for us. When we say "NO MORE PAIN" and not despise the events that we would describe as being painful but dissect and embrace them, is when things will change for us! We acquire spiritual strength when we do not allow ourselves to be consumed by emotions from our past. I have my own history of unfavorable events that I have to deal with, and I have encountered many women who cannot move past the physical, emotional and sexual abuse, betrayal and abandonment of their past.

However, when we carry that pain in our heart, it prevents us from experiencing the total joys of life. It's pertinent that you forgive once you decide that you want better for yourself. Forgiving someone doesn't imply accepting the actions from that person or anyone else that have similar intentions so that you can be used and abusive. No, it means that you are now willing to receive the healing you need. Not at all saying, "I'm ok with you talking to me like I'm nothing…I'm ok with you beating on me…I'm ok with a love one being murdered…I'm ok with you stealing from me, cheating on me, betraying me, or abandoning me."

What forgiveness is saying is that I acknowledge what the transgressor has done to me, how it made me feel, and now I must do what is required to take preventive measures so it doesn't happen again.

After reading the various stories of transformation in this book, tell yourself that it is now your time to reflect, heal and transform. Keep in mind everything that occurred in your life occurred to make you wiser, stronger, and prepare you for the person you are still to become. Extract the lesson from your experiences sis. Do not hold the pain and anger in your heart. This doesn't mean to be best friends with the person (or people) who harmed you but to make peace within yourself then move forward. Do you really want to get back at the people that transgressed against you? Then flourish! Yes sis!! Soar above the nasty names you were called, soar above that perverted person that robbed you of your childhood, soar above the sistah that left a bad taste in your mouth for sistahood, and soar above the man who broke every promise. Allow yourself to rise above the negativity and begin your healing process then assist in healing others. Yeah, that's how you get 'em. Study your culture and allow it to empower you. Walk the path of transformation with me and other sistah's and Let's Get 'Em all!

Ife Assata Fatiu
Member of PLM
Co-owner of Watoto Development Center
Co-Founder of Urban Youth Initiative Project
Founder of the Facebook Group
"Wake Up & Rise Up Sistahs"

Preface

A wise woman wishes to be no one's enemy; a wise woman refuses to be anyone's victim."

- Maya Angelou

Women Healing Other Lives Every day WHOLE Sistaz Sharing Stories of Healing and Transformation takes you on a journey into the lives of seven women who have had their share of heartache, pain, suffering and healing in this thing called life. WHOLE was inspired by the many stories of Sistaz whom I befriended at work and on social media. There were many times when I would engage in discussions and or conversations with these women that I found that most, if not all, had experienced some of the same things that I to had experienced. The women in this book have chosen to be real and transparent with you, the readers, as they give you a glimpse into their lives and the choices they made and the lessons learned from those choices. As a woman with a passion and desire to assist other women and girls in their life's journey, I wanted to give these Sistaz a platform to share their stories. These stories have begun the healing and transformation process that they need to live a life of wholeness and forgiveness and to release the hurt and anger of those who have caused them hurt and pain, as well as the hurt they have caused themselves.

What I admire about these women is that they could have easily chosen to blame others for the choices they made; however, after self-examination, they accepted their role in making those choices. It is my hope and desire that as you read these stories that they will be an encouragement and inspiration for you. Whatever choices you have made in life there is always hope that a better day will come. If you have been hurt or wounded then you can take the necessary steps to be healed and transformed.

- Angela J Barnes

Whole
Sistaz Sharing Stories of
Healing and Transformation

The Chosen Few
- Adrienne Stinson

There have been times that I wish I could fly

Spread my wings and reach the highest of heights

Soar beyond the highest of measure

Link with the forgotten and find hidden treasures

The ones, whom no longer can speak for self, take the wisdom I've gained and spread wealth

There have been times that I'd wish I could die.

Honestly speaking that's no lie.

Leave this crazy world behind and rest my mind. Seek refuge in the most high.

My intuition tells me that I'm not alone, so I know that my story is not my own.

I will share it with you. My hope is that it heals you. Many don't understand and it's ok that they don't.

The ones that do you'll know. Smiles hide pain. This I truly know. Understand that my soul speaks to you. We are the chosen few....

©Adrienne Stinson

****

Adrienne Angel Yvette Stinson is the proud mother of a 12 year old son, who started with humble beginnings. From ages 6-21 she faced a life of unstable & unpredictable circumstances in the foster care system. Life in the foster care system was unkind, traumatizing, & turbulent. But through it all she SURVIVED. At age 17 she successfully graduated from Strawberry Mansion High School in Philadelphia, PA. Shortly, after she enrolled herself into Community College of Philadelphia where she studied Theatre Arts. While at CCP she performed on stage under the direction of Dr. Ardencie Hall-Karambe', That love of Art & performing lead her to a live performing Arts experience at The Institute of Contemporary Art in Philadelphia and the Feldman Gallery in New York, New York. Today she is an accomplished writer, actress, and poet. She resides in Philadelphia with her 12 year old son.

RIDE OR DIE
- Victoria Oquendo

"Ride or Die", I whispered to the love of my life, as he turned to look at my reaction to his being sentenced to ten years, with a mandatory eighty five percent meaning he would have to serve eight years before being considered for parole or release. We met in August of 2001; we got engaged March of 2006. Between 2001 to 2006 he continuously went in and out of prison and the county jail. We were having a conversation one day and he had the nerve to get mad at me because I told him that "he lives in prison and comes home to visit". He dropped me off this particular day at the bus stop so he could do some work on my truck, he was a mechanic. He learned how to become a mechanic as an apprentice to an elder who took him under his wings and showed him how to fix cars. Before he pulled off that day he honked the horn and asked "If I had my engagement ring on"? I replied by holding up my hand and flashing my rock, he blew a kiss at me, pulled off and never reported to work. That day he smoked crack cocaine, and went on a crime spree in my truck. He committed a strong arm robbery and guess who he robbed, the very mechanic who taught him how to fix cars. After his arrest on that day he had someone contact me to tell me where my truck had been abandoned, in Newark, New Jersey. The car had a broken window, a hole cut in the seat and the radio was gone. "Ride or Die Right"? Prior to me finding my truck it had been missing for a week, I had reported it stolen to the police to cover myself as I had already knew what had happened. I was then forced into getting a new car with a car note I didn't want. My mother peace be upon her, gave me her New Ford Explorer, after her vision began to diminish due to diabetes which caused her not to be able to drive her truck any longer. Due to my mother's illness she was in and out of the hospital.

WHOLE

I'll never forget the day that my mother died; he and I were out when we got the call from the hospital that my mother was dying, and we needed to rush right to the hospital, he wanted to stop and get a bag of dope, and get high before we went. I left his ass at the cop spot and rushed to the hospital, my mother was declared dead only minutes after I got there.

We haven't been together since the day of his arrest back in 2006. As I'm riding and dying, I rode out seven of the eight year sentence, I had to fall back for a year, I was so stressed out, I developed an ulcer, I begun to experience panic and anxiety attacks because if I missed a step, a beat, a visit, a letter, a money order, a phone call or if the phone rang to many times before I answered or refusal of phone sex, there would be hell to pay. He would say if the phone rang more than twice, I was screwing someone and I had to get the Nigga off me to get to the phone, as I write this I just sit back and think about the humiliation I allowed myself to be subjugated too, from a brother in prison, not that I would have subjected myself to the same humiliation even if it were a man who wasn't behind the prison wall. While he was incarcerated I would drive 2.5 hours every weekend, there and back not to count special visits. I never did see what was so special about those visits; I traveled all over the state of New Jersey, in all types of weather to be by this man's side why he did his bid. There were times where I experienced flat tires, my car would get overheated yet I had to go to visit him no matter what the cost because I loved him and I was his ride or die chick. I recall standing in line for two hours, sometimes more waiting to see him for a thirty minute visit. I tolerated and endured nasty often flirtatious correctional officers who abused their authority, and treated the visitors like they were prisoners themselves, I felt like a prisoner and I was a prisoner of love. I was a prisoner of not only my love for him; I was a prisoner of my own foolishness, illusions and fantasies. I was found guilty for compromising my standards and principals, going against my divine intuition, I was sentence to karma. After going through hell trying to get into the prison, I would then be further subjected to even more hell, while visiting him. For instance if I came looking dressed up, hair and make-up done, which was all the time, he would really mistreat me the entire visit, the visit was more like an interrogation session. There was one incident where he accused me of deliberately choosing to sit in a certain seat so I can look and flirt with other inmates. I would be accused of writing another inmate in the same prison and he said because of what I was doing, he was the laughing stock of the prison and then he would try to clean up his behavior minutes before the visit was almost over which was his way of softening me up to keep me coming back to visit.

This brother had my route home from the prison down to a science. The minute I would pull up to my door and put my key in the door to open it the phone would ring. I would be subjected to the same torture on the phone that I endured at the prison. I would get calls from him during the middle of the night just to see if I was home; it became so bad that he accused me of being in a relationship with another man and that I had the calls forwarded so I could still answer his calls while I was lying in bed with another man. The indignities I suffered, while I was placing my life on hold waiting for him to serve his time, come home to me and we would go on with a life uninterrupted.

I remember one time I visited him at the prison he walked out on our visit before our time was up. I had to sit outside of the prison in 100 degree weather, until the joint connection bus would pick me up 2.5 hours away from home to take me back to Newark, New Jersey. I vowed I would never go back to see him again. I was so furious with him, acting out on emotions, I packed me and my son up and moved to Maryland with my sister, that didn't last but four days, my son and I were back on greyhound on our way back to New Jersey. Once I arrived back to New Jersey I had no job or apartment and my self-esteem was depleted. What little possessions that I had including my car I sold them and my 13 year old son and I ended up homeless for six months, "Ride or Die, right"? One day I was in deep thought about all that had transpired between me and him and I thought about going to see him. At that moment I said to myself Don't let the "I miss you" trick you, Don't let "I'm sorry" make you think about walking back into the party. The longer you dance with the devil, the longer you remain in hell; I had to remember I left for a reason. I had to remind myself of the stress I allowed this man and toxic relationship to cause me; I gave him my best and got his worst in return.

This prison bid was costing me a heavy price, thousands of dollars over the years in commissary, money orders, collect calls until the system changed to prepaid calls only, not to mention the countless jailhouse debts I had to settle for him, cigarettes, you name it I paid for it. What I failed to see was the true cost of what I was really paying for, I paid a dear price, for a lack of self-love and respect, no boundaries, compromising my morals and values, ignoring the red flags that presented themselves from the very first day that we met, deliberately choosing to overlook what was being presented to me. I was at a fork in the road, I now had to ask myself was I a victim or a volunteer? Was this man only giving me the love I felt that I deserved? It is said that we teach people how to treat us, did I really teach this man that he can mistreat me?, due to the ride or die mentality I developed vowing to ride or die while crossing oceans for a man, who wouldn't even jump a puddle for me. I met my ex August of 2001, his car ran out of gas and I helped him and the woman he was dating at the time, get gas for their car. He pushed up on me right in front of her; he even went as low as to ask her for the pen and paper that he used to get my telephone number. What was I thinking? He called me the day after I gave him my number from her house, while she was out. He told me I could call the house and just say I was his cousin Angel. I played the game, calling another woman's house, lying about my identity; didn't I see that this was an utter disrespect to this woman, and to myself? NO, I only saw what I wanted. Lies will always be bitter in the end, no matter how sweet you made it in the beginning. We would talk for hours. He would tell me how bad she treated him, how she was a monster. He told me everything she wasn't, and didn't or wouldn't do, so I sought to be everything she wouldn't be, you know RIDE OR DIE. I had to save him from the woman who he described as a monster; time would soon reveal later who the real monster was. I saved her from the monster by inviting the monster in my home, my bed and in my head. Who was going to save me from the monster? I will never forget that day when I was speaking to his ex who to this very day is one of my best, dearest and closet friends thanked me for taking the monster from her house. Although it hurt it was the best thing that could have happened, she said, I only did for her what she didn't have the courage or ability to do for herself, everything he did to her, he did to me, and after all, didn't I jump in her shoes? The same woman who I showed no respect for fed me and the man who left her, because I couldn't keep money, because I was supporting his drug habit. She listened to me for countless hours as I cried about him and his poor choices and drug addiction. My life was spiraling out of control. I remember her trying to warn me about him, but because I wasn't ready to hear the truth I chalked it up to she was hating because I took her man. I was too ignorant and too immature to see the divine warnings that were being sent to me, one of many that kept coming to me.

When you think you're in love you only see what you want to see. We fight for the things we aren't supposed to have and then complain about the pain it brought us. One of the many lessons I learned during this very emotional and trying season of my life was, the way you get them (the man/woman) is the same way you lose them. After he paroled out and I made the decision to not be at the gate when he was released February of 2013, two days later, he was already moved in another woman's house, where did she come from? I never crossed paths with another woman the entire eight year bid, I was his only visitor and support system. Later I found out the woman he was with was a state employee, the van driver for the halfway house he was in. Word was she was easy, had low self-esteem, and you could "come up off of her". So like the predator he is, she set his plan B in motion. I wanted to warn her, I wanted her to know that she was about to invite a demon into her home into her life, but experience taught me she would only say I was hating, and bitter because we weren't together and he was with her. The same thing I thought his ex was trying to do to me, to get me to leave him alone. He met this woman, when he got to the half-way house. During the time that he was incarcerated I had slipped and fell in the grocery store, this resulted in me breaking my leg in several places which left me wheel chair bound, unable to walk or work, bottom line to him I guess I was of no use and couldn't' run behind him. Keeping true to my ride or die mantra, I made arrangements to meet up with the women of other inmates, and they would help me get to visit and drive my car. It was hard being with these females, bonding and getting to know them and knowing that I would see other women coming to visit their men on the days they had to work or didn't make their visit. I saw the game that was being ran down on these unsuspecting sisters. I had yet to see that I was being shown something here, that they were mirror reflections of where I was or going to be. Now that he was in the halfway house the game changes a little, now he could wear street clothing, he could shine, we could deviate when he got a pass to go look for work. We could have sex, in yards, parks, parked cars, no time for anything more than a quickie. When we did have sex he was like an animal he had become a sexual beast. I dreaded to see the caller id, if it would be him, all he wanted was phone sex, to talk about it, hear it, watch it, and smell it, any and all roads led back to sex. The final destruction of the relationship I thought I was in, was when he wanted me to fulfill his fantasy, a fantasy that consisted of me sleeping with a well-endowed man, let him call the house, hide the phone and let him hear me have sex, and he told me that "I better not hold back" is this a dream, he wanted me to sex another man and let him listen, WTF? I asked, I knew the moment of truth arrived, how was I going to reason with his animal behavior this time? Whose fault it would be, who I could blame for him being the way he was. This man couldn't love me, he wanted to pimp me out to choose who, what, where and how I slept with other men. It got so bad, that he began to get a nasty attitude and demanding that this had to happen, that the future of us relied on me fulfilling his fantasy, I felt so low, so devalued, so unprotected and cheap. It was clear that I was not respected or appreciated; I had to stop asking why he kept doing the hurtful things he had been subjecting me to and start asking, why did I keep allowing it to happen? Under the illusion I created I thought we were compatible, that we had so much in common. There were lots of synchronicity in our relationship; what I realized thirteen years later that of all the likeness we shared, we did not share the same morals and values I outgrew him. While he was doing his time, and I was serving my own time with myself and growing and changing, he used to say to me all the time during my visits to the prison "you changed Vic", "your changing on me". I used to deny it, as if change is a bad thing or something to be ashamed of, I was afraid that he wouldn't like the new me, that he would leave if I wasn't the same Vic he left eight years ago. The truth of the matter is I wasn't the same Vic. It started with the death of my mother, my fiancé going to prison, my company liquidating and my car being repossessed. I exhausted my unemployment benefits, lost my apartment, ended up homeless, unable to secure employment I ended back up on Public Assistance living out of a hotel for six months with my son. It was during this time I began to search for myself, it was during this time I learned that in my most trying years, this man was never there for me, he was either in jail, serving some sort of time, sniffing dope or just down right emotionally unavailable to me, he was a taker, he took more than he gave, he lied to me more then he told me the truth, he made me cry more then he made me laugh, he hurt me more then he healed me, he showed just enough, he gave me just enough, to see that his needs always got met while keeping me around wanting and waiting for the next rare random act of kindness or love, I was loving him while losing me. He gave me just enough to have a stronghold on me, enough to get me to ride or die. I endured emotional, psychological and physical abuse, while holding on to every word he said, in spite of the fact that his actions were not in alignment with the words he spoke or the countless broken and false promises he made. I needed help, but you can't save a damsel, if she loves her distress, and I was in love with the cause and cure for my pain and suffering, trying to be mindful of what to throw away, push away and thinking hard before walking away, the question I had to ask myself "what was I loosing here'? Was I really sad over the thought of moving on and no longer allowing myself to be treated like a doormat? Why was my heart so heavy? Why did I feel like I was handed down a death sentence? Was I going to continue to allow this man to take me for granted? Had I finally reach the point where I was tired of feeling unappreciated? I was accepting crumbs from a man when I knew I wanted and desired the entire loaf?

One of the biggest mistakes we as women make when it comes to a man is waiting around and thinking he will change. You can't expect something different from someone who hasn't done anything to change, sometimes, it's not that people change; it's that they show themselves for who they truly are. This man had been showing me who he was and who I was, I just hadn't been paying attention. Refusing to play the victim role, I had to own up to my part of this insanity. I had to get up from a table where love was no longer being served. Considering how hard it is to change yourself, I understood what little chance I had of trying to change him, the more lies he told the more truth I had to tell myself, the more he denied me, the more I had to go within to give to myself, the more he made me cry, I had to make myself laugh even more, the more he lacked, the more I learned to give to myself. A fact of life is some will never care about who they hurt, as long as they get what they want. Anything that hurts you can teach you, and if it keeps hurting you, it's because you haven't learned. Respecting yourself enough to walk away from anything that no longer serves you, grow you, or make you happy is no easy task, especially when one of the hardest things I ever had to learn to let go of what I thought was real. You can't lose what you never had, you can't keep what's not yours and you can't hold on to something that doesn't want to stay. I felt like an addict when it came to this man, the strongest drug that exist for a human being is another human being. If he makes you lose your family, friends, confidence, self-esteem, and happiness, then you need to lose him. A strong woman that won't compromise her self-respect can get any real man to love her, but if she becomes a pet, a slave, a floor mat or a push over, he will play with her heart and then leave her for a woman who will make him respect her. It was clear that this man had no respect for me; even clearer was the fact that I had no self-respect for myself for allowing this to transpire. Looking back, I can see the many times, the universe was attempting to remove this man from my life. I had many ways out, and yet I still had that ride or die mentality, and it would have to take an act from G_D to remove him because I was so caught up, I surely couldn't walk away, even when everything within me was screaming for me to let go, I was stuck in the familiar, the fantasy, the illusion that I created in my mind, while he was playing I was seriously riding and dying a slow death. I even see my accident resulting in a broken leg as a way being provided out, and a beautiful blessing in disguise. My broken leg was symbolic of just how broken I was and that I was not standing firmly upon my two feet; you know stand for something or fall for anything.

I have come to learn that we don't attract to us who we want, we attract to us who we are. My ex was a mirror reflection of me, an extreme male version of me, when you point the finger, there will be 3 fingers pointing right back at you, when you think everything else is someone else's fault you will suffer a lot, when you realize that everything springs only from yourself, you will learn both peace and joy. My loyalty to my ex had become a form of enslavement. I thought he was my soul mate. I use to think that maybe I wasted thirteen years of my life being in this toxic relationship. No relationship is ever a waste of time, if it didn't bring me what I wanted; it taught me what I didn't want. People think a soul mate is your perfect fit, isn't that what everyone wants?, but the truth of the matter is, a true soul mate is a mirror, this person shows you everything that is holding you back, this is the person who brings you to your own attention, so you can change your life. A true soul mate is probably the most important person you'll ever meet, because they tear down your walls, and smack you awake. A soul mates purpose is to shake you up, tear apart your ego, little, by little, show you your obstacles and addictions, break your heart open so new light can get in, make you so out of control that you have to change your life. My life was so out of control, the pain became so great, I only had two choices, use it as a motivator or stay stagnated. I decided to get better not bitter, never make something you're everything because when it's gone, you'll feel as though you have nothing. The moment of truth had arrived, I was done. Learning to let go of what you thought was real was hard, learning to love myself and walk away was even harder. I learned that my behavior with men comes from being abandoned by my father, growing up without a male role model or father figure in the home. My father was an adulterous womanizer and abuser, he shot my mother, right in front of us as children; he was a drug dealing, emotionally unavailable man, sounds familiar? I'm in a new place in life, for the first time, I'm joyful; I have an awesome relationship with my three children. There was one point in my life where I thought the seeds I bore hated me, they disrespected me about as much as I did myself and as much as they seen the men who came and left disrespect me. I have an awesome relationship with myself. At the time of this writing my ex is still calling asking for another chance. When you fall back they crawl back claiming they want it all back. I told him the last time he called to feel me out. I gave him thirteen years of my life; he can't have another thirteen seconds. I put a block on my phone so that he cannot reach me. Hating him was draining me and a complete waste of energy. He continues to call to beg for sex on a regular. After all I have done and who I was to him all he misses is the sex life we had.

The writing of this story has been a pivotal turning point of my life and healing. Reading and reminiscing over the toxic relationship that I had with men and myself, saying all the things I never got to say to him, and the questions I never got ask, you know those crazy thoughts of all the things that you could have said that comes to you after you hang up the phone. I no longer care to know why things happened the way they did, I've gotten with full acceptance of the way things unfolded. I've given myself the closure that I begged him for months to give me. I wanted him to admit verbally, what his actions was showing me, that he didn't care about me, why did I need to hear it? He didn't tell me he didn't want me, he showed me. No matter the reason or logic behind our parting ways, in hind sight, it was for the best and divinely orchestrated. Sometimes a man's purpose in a woman's life is to help her become a better woman for another man. I am a good woman, but no matter how good of a woman you are, you'll never been good enough for a man who isn't ready. At the time of this writing I am currently single and just working on being content with myself and loving me unconditionally. I have not given up on love or being in a healthy relationship. I know that my husband is out there and in the meantime while I wait on him as he is waiting on me I will continue to work on my healing and transformation.

****

Victoria Paula Oquendo, was born July 1968, the second oldest of four daughters, a native New Yorker, Victoria's mother fled New York with her three children after, being shot by their father in front of them. Her mother settled in New Jersey. Victoria grew up in a strict matriarchal religious household. At the age of fourteen Victoria began to rebel against her mother, she moved out at the age of sixteen, dropped out of high school in the 12th grade, in an attempted to hide a pregnancy. Victoria is a single mother of three, a 27 year old daughter, two sons 26 & 15.

Victoria struggled being a young single mother, grappling with irresponsibility, drug addiction, rape, poverty, homelessness, mental breakdowns, short jail stints, domestic violence and a suicide attempt. The year 2009 would be a turning point in her life, as she sought to gain knowledge of herself; making heritage and religious discoveries that have contributed to the woman she is today.

After taking two years to soul search, she birthed "Changing Faces" channeling pain through art, she became a talented face painter, Also "PACT" was birth "Protecting All Children Together is a 501 c3 nonprofit organization, educating urban children about human trafficking and child exploitation and abduction, in loving memory of Avonte Oquendo, the autistic child who went missing from his school, who's body parts later were found along the East, NY, River. She also launched "Sister with Scents" a homemade all natural soap venture, which is doing well. Victoria is also the Administrator for the Masjidd, The Islamic Center of Passaic/Paterson, where she over sees Sadaqa (charity) Inc, a local food pantry that serves about four hundred families a month, with emergency food bags, as well as oversee the resource room, where she assists with resumes, housing matters or any form of social injustice.

The Rise Of The Phoenix
- Yahtiley Phoenix
(aka) Brande Ward

One of the hardest things that I had to do was fight for my life, between October and November 2004. In April 2004 I was in a major car accident and suffered severe head trauma. This incident sparked a change of events in my life. The accident was so bad the fire department had to cut me out of a mangled car. After the car accident, I was transported to the hospital by ambulance. After lots of test I was diagnosed with bruised ribs and a slight concussion, according to the doctor's report. A month later I had my first seizure and was told I had epilepsy due to head trauma from the car accident. I asked my primary care doctor if I needed test done before taking Tegretol, an anti – seizure medicine prescribed. I also asked what the side effects of the Tegretol were. My doctor said the worst case scenario would be headaches. I figured I could handle headaches if the medicine would take away my seizures. My doctor claimed to be the expert on this medicine so I trusted her medical expertise. Little did I know this was the beginning stage of the fight for my life. Six months later I had to schedule an emergency doctor's appointment, because of the blisters on my hands and arms. I was also concerned because I had a burning sensation throughout my body. My doctor just said I had a rash, but I knew that something else was wrong. Several days later my skin looked, felt, and smelled horrible. I went to the hospital and was admitted. I stayed in the hospital in October 2004 for seven days. The doctors did not know what was wrong with me. It took a nurse to diagnose me with Stevens-Johnson Syndrome (SJS). The medicine I was taking Tegretol caused a serve allergic reaction which caused an internal fever resulting in burns. I was given different tests and the Tegretol was lowered in its dose and changed to Carbamazepine.

The Tegretol should be discontinued due to allergic reactions. Each day the burns got worse and multiplied. By November 2004 I had burns over 90 percent of my body. I went back to my doctor and she continued to say I had a rash. At this point, I could not see because I had mucus and scabs on my eye lids. I could barely open my eyes. Another doctor informed my doctor that I should be hospitalized or there could be a malpractice lawsuit. I was then pre-admitted to a local hospital. While I was there the doctor placed the I.V. through a catheter in my groin area. I asked the doctor what the funny odor from my body was and he asked if I knew what burning flesh smelled like? My body was a crematorium. During my second hospitalization my burns were more severe, and I suffered brain damage from a high fever. This lead to Peterson's Syndrome which is a brain virus. I remember also dying on several occasions while suffering from SJS. After being released from the hospital, I went to a nursing /rehab center for several weeks. While there I received care for my burns and had to learn how to walk. I was temporarily in a wheel chair. I also had to re teach myself to write again. To this day I have problems with reading, writing, comprehension and memory recall.

A month before I suffered from SJS I saw a news story about a girl who died from SJS. She was given children's Tylenol; because of this news story I was able to understand what was going on with me. I still get outbreaks of blisters and burns often. My husband is the best; he stays up late at night when I am in pain, misses work to take care of me, and has been with me at the hospital. I love him for all the love, care, and sacrifices; Robert Myer Ward Jr. Hashima Umoja Rudo makes for me!!!

When I was sick I drew strength and prayed to my African and Native-American Ancestors. My Native-American name is Yahtiley Faith Keeper Sacajawea Phoenix, it means "she who heals herself on her journey will rise from the ashes of adversity and will heal the world". The burns from the SJS burned a **Y** in my nose. This is my battle scar!!! I know that I am resistant and determined. One of the major things that I took away from this experience is to be in charge of your health. Ask a million questions to your doctor; do research about medical conditions, medicine and side effects. I survived for a reason and that is to tell my story. For me the journey is not over it has only begun.

"I am the rise of the Phoenix"

****

Yahtiley Faithkeeper Sacajawea Phoenix / Brande Michelle Ward, has an Associates of Arts Degree in General Studies from the Community College of Baltimore County Catonsville Campus. She majored in Political Science, Sociology, and she has a Certification in Early Childhood Education. In 2001 Yahtiley received a Bachlor of Science in Government and Public Policy from the University of Baltimore. She also worked on a Master of Arts in Legal and Ethical studies. Yahtiley believes in helping others and putting them first. She received a certification to be an Advocate for People with H.I.V. and A.I.D.S. on October 3, 2012 through the L.E.A.P. sixteen program. During L.E.A.P. sixteen Yahtiley graduated with Honors and received the highest award given the Cleo Award, which shows leadership and advocacy skills Currently, Yahtiley is an Advocate for People with H.I.V. and A.I.D.S.. She sits as a member on the Continuum of Care Committee, which is a Sub-Committee of the Greater Baltimore H.I.V. Health Services Planning

Council which she has been a member of since 2012. Yahtiley has been an advocate and worked in the H.I.V. and A.I.D.S. Community for 25 years, since the age of 15. She also is an advocate for the mentally ill and is a Consumer Advisory Board Executive Member for Advocate Support Services. She is also a Member of N.A.M.I, the National Alliance of the Mentally Ill.

In Yahtiley's spare time she loves to attend Afrikan Awareness and Critical Thinking Study Classes, and spending time with her Ma'at Sisters, an Afrikan Centered Sisterhood. Yahtiley resides in Baltimore, Maryland with her husband, the love of her life, Hashima Umoja Rudo/ Robert Myer Ward Jr. and her beloved nephew-son Raymond C. Jefferson Jr.

Out Of My Mind Just In Time
- Gorthie Hopkins

By looking at me you could never tell what I went through. The year was 2001, as I remember the first time I tried cocaine it was very new to me, because I was once a pot head I told my friends and family I would never indulge in something so powerful and addictive as cocaine, never say never.

I was an undercover coke head that had all the comforts of home: clothes, money and a car. Everything good; including a family to come home to. The only thing that was missing was a steady man in my life. I'm not sure, maybe that was the problem I was trying to fill a void. One of my family members turned me on to cocaine or should I say got me hooked on cocaine. I must admit I loved it; the high it gave, then the numbness I felt in my mouth, it was like speed, it kept you up and going. It came in handy for work when I had long hours at the job. I used cocaine for 11 years, or more. I even got bold with it; snorting at the job in the restroom. I never got caught because I was too clever for that, no one was the wiser. I kept it hidden back then; my appearance didn't change and I was the same happy go lucky person I had always been.

The only people that knew were my mom and my family, and they were not telling. When I was using back then I thought I was the coolest thing around; I stayed fly with my clothes, had a job, and did not ask anyone to support my habit. I had it all figured out; however, in the long run it hit me like a slow bullet. At the time I never realized the world wind I was in, so I continued as nothing happened. I would say about three years in to me using I began to want more; I was hooked. I needed a bigger stash and a better quality. I used because I was bored. I was raised in a small town practically all of my life. I knew everyone there. We had beaches, parks, and movies it was just that something was missing; now that I look back and think about what it was the energy no energy what so ever, everyone I knew was either dead, had family that died, were in jail or went crazy. I noticed all of that, but like I did back then I easily dismissed it from my mind; I just wanted to get high. The higher I got the better I felt, that is what cocaine does it numbs your feelings. I was on cloud nine sometimes in a world of make believe, my own world no one could enter if I did not give them permission. I became very selective with the people I hung with. After all, people talked and I did not want certain people around, I had to be careful. I had a good paying job at a very reputable hospital and I could not risk losing it. I needed the job to support everything I held dear; the cocaine, kids, house, car and clothes.

When I used cocaine, I felt strange yet capable I had never felt like this, nothing ever felt like this before. I was in a weird kind of wonderful; no you can't change me that was my motto. I would always say I'm grown, as if saying that gave me the right to snort cocaine; another name for it was fish scale or P funk. Supporting my habit was easy back then everybody and they mama was selling it. I had good connections, friends in high places. A friend of a friend kept me straight I did not want for nothing. If I did not have it I could always bet on my friends or one of my family members having a snort or two. I was high all the time coming and going, I lived for it and yet I thought I was fine.

One day I remember my mom sitting me down and talking to me about it, she asked me straight out "are you using cocaine" I said yes, when I look back on that day I literally want to cry now; I really hurt her so much when I replied to her and said yes, I never will forget that look she gave me; it was as if she had did something to make me do such a thing as to turn to a drug called cocaine. She could not say anything else, she just got up from the kitchen table and left. I just sat there stuck on stupid. I was ready for her to come back and preach like she always did because I was ready to say I am grown, I can do what I want. As I look back now I think to myself why didn't she curse me out? Or why didn't she give me the long speech like she always did? Maybe she thought I had it all figured out or maybe she knew I was going through a phase in my life and that I would stop one day.

That day I wish my mom would have yelled, screamed or cursed me out; I know I hurt her but at the time I did not care who I hurt. I left to go get high. Every time I would go out to a bar or house party cocaine was there. One time when I went to the bar there was this brotha there sitting in the VIP area, I was happy to see him sitting at the table white lines, P. funk in the air, razors on the table with rolled up fifty dollar bills and what have you. The music was pumping in the background the people were loud and having a good time, we ordered drinks after drinks. We felt no pain, no one had a worry in the world. The bar scene drew in all kinds of people there were doctors, lawyers and politicians; as they say cocaine is the rich man's high; from what I experienced it was. These rich men had money and I had the time. If I was not at work I would hang around the Italian guys, surgeons and lawyers; you would not believe that people with a reputable profession such as the aforementioned did cocaine. These people walked around as if they were celebrities driving Cadillac's, Lincoln MKZ, BMW's, and they were crazy about me. They knew my mom and my family and anything my mom or family wanted they could have because of the beautiful woman I was and that made them and me feel powerful.

When in the company of these professional men I rarely had to pay for a drink at the bar when I went out to party. When the men saw me and my sisters they would set up the bar. The men used to always say how beautiful and attractive that I was and my sisters would use my looks to get what we wanted. My sisters would say "so and so is watching you go ask him if he has some blow". I would do it, I was invincible, I could do anything. Sure enough he had what we needed Diamonds; we called it that because if you can get the good stuff it would look like tiny diamonds shimmering on top of white dust. I played the game well not knowing what I was in for in the long run. This kind of behavior went on for years and years a whirl wind of charades and although I was caught up in the game I still took care of my responsibilities. I still paid my rent, car insurance and provided for my kids. I had to keep that part of my life in line so that no one would be the wise, especially the school system, they never found out about my double life.

    I was getting better and better at hiding my true identity.

    Autumn came around and it started to get chilly, the leaves were changing so beautifully. This is the time to stay in and cook soups and stews, I was never big on eating so I always watched what I ate in this particular phase of my life instead of losing weight I started to gain weight even though I was a coke head I didn't look the part that's the reason why so many did not know that I was using. Growing up as a young girl even into my adult years I was always thin. The weight gain was due to me going through menopause and when you go through menopause you tend to gain weight, along with the weight gain came depression, a bad attitude, ego and disrespect towards people. There is a price to pay when you abuse narcotics of any kind. I don't care what and how your using you will pay the price and the price is usually your conscience.

Over the years of using cocaine I started to go downhill; I started to loose knowledge of self, my energy depleted, I became superficial, and I started to date Italians, the ones that had the good cocaine supply and the money to back it up. My habit and my head was getting bigger I needed more money to support my habit. During this time I became intimate with a very reputable and prestigious lawyer, we were like two peas in a pod. We hung out together I had him and he had me lock, stock and barrel. Because of his prestigious background he was like a celebrity and I felt on top of the world, when people would see us coming they would high five and ask him "what's good" and shit like that, he would be grinning from ear to ear while looking back at me, I was always dressed to impress, my hair stayed styled and I kept manicured nails. I had it liked that, I felt important and beautiful; little did I know my mentality was so ugly, phony and shallow on the surface I knew I was the shit but discreetly I started to feel sick of myself because mentally and physically I was gone. Anything I needed, drugs or money, all I had to do was ask and he would give it to me as long as I was giving up the cookies, in other words having sex with him. If I needed money or the car fixed he was right there to help save the day, three of four hundred dollars was nothing to him, and he never asked questions about why I needed it. The way I saw it was he had what I needed and I had what he wanted and so you can say we both used each other for what we wanted.

    My family knew him and my kids respected him and they could get anything they wanted from him as well. Once you have a habit as I once did you get smart on thinking how you're going to support your habit, I knew what I was doing, he was my stash sort of speak, my put away for a rainy day man. Not only that, but he was married with a family. His wife used to come to my house and eat with me and she used cocaine too. I am not happy about that but that's the game, you lose your sense of pride and do just about anything for that shit, our superficial romance lasted about three years, she never found out.

As the months and years went by I began to feel sick and tired, sick and tired of seeing the same people going to the same clubs. I began to feel at my lowest, I guess I was coming to a point where I was getting tired of the games and the life that comes with snorting cocaine. I still indulged in cocaine, I just could not let it go like that, it had a hold on me in some strange way. We were connected, I know it may sound crazy but at the time it didn't to me. Cocaine would take me to a height which I felt invincible and powerful.

My family started to see less of me, they would call me sometimes and I would not answer the phone, I just wanted to be alone with my thoughts. I knew if I picked up the phone what they were going to say and I did not want to hear it I just wanted them to stay out of my business and my way. I was in command of this ship and I would snap at anyone who would try to detour it. How was anybody going to tell me how to do me, I was not having it. After years of using cocaine my body began to shut down, I did not want to see anyone; I stopped partying and stayed in the house more. I was so tired of the lifestyle that I was living; eventually I got so sick that I could not move, I was so fatigued and my face started to break out. When I looked in the mirror I looked ugly; I had no appetite and some days I would just stay in the bed all day long I had no energy to do anything.

      Months had passed and I had stopped using cocaine. During that time I became mean and hateful towards my family, children and friends, I didn't like myself and the person I had become. What I didn't realize was I was going through withdrawals, I was sick too sick to even want anymore; I became so sick that a big cyst appeared on my back, I was in chronic pain, so much pain that I could not even sleep. I went to the doctor and he had to lance it. All the cocaine and garbage that I had put in my body over the years, was now coming out of my system. I fell into a deep depression and I actually wanted to commit suicide. I was alone most of the time anyway on top of that I was feeling that my family didn't love me, I had no man and I got fired from my job in the lab department at the hospital, I had hit rock bottom. My consciousness was gone I had no reason to live; the only way for me to stop feeling the way I did was to take my own life.

I remember thinking how should I do it? I thought about the pills that the doctor had prescribed for my depression if I took a lot of those that would do it. During this time I could not sleep, I started to have nightmares, crazy dreams of the devil and all kinds of creatures they were trying to take them with me full force. My house started to feel very negative to me and evil; it was a super natural force in there, but it wasn't stronger than me. Every time it would appear I would pray to Allah and repeat the words "I banish you", and it would leave me alone. Sleep was impossible all I wanted was just a good night's sleep and it was not happening. I was drowning into the depths of a lower consciousness of hell.

In 2011 I began to watch Trinity Broadcasting Network (TBN) every morning. After watching this I began to pray more and more each day. Although I never believed in the bible in hind sight it was the inspiration from TBN that I needed to pull me back from the depths of hell. During this time I did not want anyone to visit me; I just wanted to stay to myself. I really needed this time alone to begin to pick up the pieces of my shattered life to come back to reality. After, I came out of the hospital following the surgery on my back to remove the cyst the same people who I alienated where the same people that nursed me back to health, my family and my children. While recovering from surgery I continued to watch TBN. I really became fascinated by Bishop Clarence E. McClendon, he literally brought me back to life with his sermons. I started to get my strength and dignity back, then my faith in myself again; my whole being just bristled up and

I started feeling better day by day.

I remember one day I said to myself that I need another laptop, the one I had before I sold for cocaine. Wow! Did I just say that? Yes I did, I sold my soul back then, and lost my dignity and self-respect. As I sit here and write and reveal my shame to you I wear it like a tattoo, there must have been an angel by my side, I was holding on to the reigns of something much bigger on this physical plane and it didn't let me go either. I was supposed to be here, for what reason I will never get to learn on this planet.

In June 2013, as I began to heal myself from within I decided to leave my home town and re-locate to a different city so that I could find myself and collect my thoughts. I had a best friend here who I thought was my best friend, she turned out to be my worst enemy, that is in the past now. Today I am much happier, healthy, wiser, and kinder. I never felt stronger and more confident than I do today. I met a beautiful single man and I am now in a healthy relationship. I lost my mind and came to my senses. I am thankful for my struggles because without them I would not have stumbled across my strengths. What inspired me to write is what I see in everyday life, the struggles that everyday people go through. I always wanted to be a writer but it took a back seat to my singing which was my first love. I am a woman of many hats.

In closing I would just like to leave you with this quote "If I knew anything at all, it's that a wall is just a wall and nothing more at all; it can be broken down" - Assata Shakur.

****

Gorthie B. Hopkins G.B.H was born and raised in Uttica NY. She is the mother of four and grandmother of eight, a singer, writer, actor and activist. She is currently working on her debut book which will be released 2015. She currently resides in Atlanta, Georgia.

It Made Me Strong
- Bianca Bostic

It was April 21, 214, when my mother called me at work. I could tell as soon as I answered the phone that something was wrong, but I was not expecting this. She said that she was not feeling well and started to cry. I said I was on my way home. The entire car ride home I cried, prayed, and bargained with God that whatever was wrong with my mom I could take as long as she was ok. It was the longest walk up the front four steps, and an even longer walk to the den once I was in the house. She sat there in the dining room chair and I knew that it was worst then I even expected. She told me that she had stage two breast cancer, and my heart broke. I have been divorced and suffered a miscarriage, but the pain of my mother telling me that she had breast cancer was all consuming. I could see her mouth moving and I wanted to hear what she was saying but I just could not. There was this intense echoing and ringing in my ears and I just could not comprehend what was happening. I sat there across from my mother and just thought of how different our lives would be.

My mom and I have the best relationship ever, we even joke about being twins. Even though we look nothing alike, and she is a lot more outgoing then I am, and we act different most of the time, we still have many of the same thoughts. We go to concerts together, movies and shopping of course. Growing up I did not have many friends and I could always count on my mom to offer me more than just mom support, but she was my friend. Even through those rough teenage years, she loved and supported me. When I was nineteen and too afraid to tell I was pregnant, her she loved me through it all. Don't get me wrong she was mad at me and didn't speak to me for a while, but from the moment my daughter was born until today she has been a mother to us both when I did not know how. So, to have my friend tell me she had cancer I was just in shock.

Cancer is a relentless monster. It ravages your spirit and your soul and takes no prisoners. From the time my mom told me it was doctor's appointments, scans, tests, all in preparation for the *red devil* – the aptly named chemotherapy drug she was supposed to take. I went with my mother to every appointment, test, and scan. I didn't know what else to do, but I knew that the least I could do was be there for her. It was amazing that my mother who had always been so strong now appeared so fragile and afraid. Me, I was supposed to be the strong one? I could not image being as strong for her as she had been for me. After all I still cried during chick-flicks, sometimes I was afraid to be alone, and since my own diagnosis of Multiple Sclerosis less than two-years ago, I felt like I was always walking against the current. Now it was my time to step up and be the strong one. Could I do it? Could I be brave, supportive, encouraging, compassionate and strong? Of course I could, well I guess I did not really have a choice right. This was my life, my new reality, my new normal – my mommy had cancer.

During her MRI she discovered that she was claustrophobic, so I went into the MRI machine with her and held her hand. I did it, I was nervous and prayed the entire time for strength and courage but I did it. I was there for her and I think that my strength helped her to get through it. We went for more test and scans. Finally we the culminating appointment, were we learned the treatment plan. Six months of treatment – four months of chemotherapy, a mastectomy and radiation is what they told us. The doctor said ten years ago, they would have done a mastectomy right away, but modern medicine has seen better results from this course of treatment. I thank God for the many women, who had to suffer from this terrible illness to save my mother.

I went online and learned everything that I could; *I*

guess the internet is good for something. I researched the doctors, the hospital, even the pharmaceutical company. If I could not take the cancer from her I could at least make sure she knew all there was to know. I prayed, but not for me, not even for her not to be sick, it was too late for that. Instead, I prayed for God to give her strength and comfort through it. I prayed for God to put her in the hands of the best doctors – who would know and care for her as a person and not just as a patient. I prayed that He would take away the fear and any pain, physical and emotional, and help her not feel alone. I tried to comfort her, but I knew like she did that when we closed our eyes we were alone with our thoughts, our fears and our regrets.

Regrets, what a painful thing. They make you wish that you did things different, that you lived life different, that you said something different. I realized that instead of regretting the things I had said or did that I was now ashamed of I could live my life better and not do those things anymore. I could open myself up for receiving and giving love. I could learn to love and forgive wholeheartedly. I could even learn to love those who pained me. I could reach out to my father and forgive him for all the pain and hurt even without him asking to be forgiven. It is quite ironic that it takes a major medical illness to make you realize how valuable life is. We only get one chance at this life – we should enjoy it not regret it.

My mom is two months into her treatment. She has lost her hair and many days she lost her spirit, but she never lost her faith, and she will never lose my support. We talk all of the time, which is not different then before she was sick. I am with her at every treatment to make her smile. Sure right now we are not shopping or hanging out as much, but hanging-in is just as great.

From this experience I have learned to love better. I have learned to give better. I am a better friend, a better mother, a better sister and daughter – not just to my mother, but also to my father. Most importantly I have learned to be better. While cancer is an unwanted guest in our lives and our family, it has shed some light on the dark spots in our life. Cancer showed us how quickly life can change and how important it is to cherish it. Cancer has shown my family how important living a great life the first time is and not replaying your life in regret. Cancer has shown my family the importance of being there for each other. While I wish my mom would have never gotten cancer, I thank God for the love and support I have been able to give her. I thank God for the ability to show her even a small percentage of the love she has always shown me. I guess I am strong after all.

****

Bianca Bostic is the mother of a vivacious eleven-year-old names Jocelyn. Bianca attends the University of Maryland University College where she will receive a Bachelor of Science degree in Management Studies in May 2015. Bianca is a member of the Maryland Higher Education Council where she advocates for the educational advancement of minority adult students. She volunteers in her local community and walks annually with the Multiple Sclerosis Society to help STOMP OUT MS! *Bianca's mom is doing well!!!*

When Pain Becomes your Friend
- Angela Barnes

Throughout my life I have suffered much trauma, heartache, and pain. I used to think that pain and suffering was my first and last name. Adversity was a common occurrence in my life from conception and being a fetus in my mother's womb. My mother was eighteen years old at the time with two other children and then she conceived me. When I was still in my mother's womb she was shot in her stomach; the bullet missed me by several inches. Although I survived the bullet womb the trauma from that experience caused me to be a really sick infant and my mom was not able to properly take care of me. She left me with a family that was close to ours and who were able to provide and take better care of me.

As a little girl I was molested; at the age of nineteen I was raped and as an adult I was committed to the psychiatric ward on three different occasions. It was March 2006, and I had just left a church after being a member there for three years; it turned out to be a cult. The pastor at the time was a very young, intelligent, and charismatic man that used manipulation and control to oversee the congregants in the church. Well, after leaving that church I fell into a deep depression, I had been awakened to the deception, manipulation, control and fear tactics used by the pastor. I really looked up to this man as a spiritual leader and advisor only to be wounded and abused spiritually by him. It was not enough to be wounded, hurt, and abused by those in the world as I did with the molestation and rape; but to come into the house of God that is supposed to be a place of refuge and healing for the pain was just too much for me to bear. This experience landed me in the psychiatric ward and that was the first occasion.

While at the psychiatric ward the doctor explained to me that I had been holding in all of those experiences for so very long while trying to keep my head above water and deal with the day to day hustle and bustle of making a comfortable life for myself and my two children, and it was just too much for the mind to handle. I just sank. I was tired of being the strong black woman, I just did not want to be strong anymore that I just had a nervous breakdown or a psychotic episode, as the doctor identified my experience. After my release from the hospital I had two relapses three months apart because I had stopped taking the prescribed medication. One of them was Risperdal which is one of many anti-psychotic medications that helps with mental illnesses. However, it made me feel like a zombie; I felt tired and spaced out all of the time. It was a struggle for me to get out of bed, to go to work, clean my house or do other day to day activities that I was doing before the nervous breakdown. The last psychotic episode was December 2010, the doctor said that I would have to take this medication for the rest of my life. I said to myself oh no way, the way this medication makes me feel there is no way that I would be taking these for the rest of my life. I began to do research and look for alternatives methods to help me with what the psychiatrist had diagnosed me with schizophrenia. Go figure! These synthetic drugs can cause bladder/kidney infections and all sorts of other ailments. It has been four years since I stop taking that medication and I feel actually great. If I can take a pause here for a moment I do not advise anyone who may be taking this medication to stop using it until you have talked with your doctor as every situation is different. During my research on what schizophrenia was I realized that the people who suffered from this illness had certain symptoms that I did not experience and to my knowledge no one in my family had a mental illness. Today I am living a happy and successful life without taking the medication. I am eating right, exercising, taking better care of myself and I am now starting to look out for me. I think about all the times that I would suppress my feelings, wants and needs at the expense of making other's happy only to be hurt/wounded by those same people. I tell you after you experience so much pain and suffering in your life it's like when people hurt or wound you it's feels as if you have just become immune to the pain. I lived most of my life like that and I refuse to continue to live that way. Today, I have made a conscious decision to start taking better care of myself mentally, emotionally, and physically. I do not allow people to enter into my personal space where they can hurt me. Moreover, I realized that I had put people on pedestals and felt that they could not do any wrong. Therefore, I take responsibility as well. You may ask have I put up a wall where no one can hurt or cause me pain again? The answer is a resounding no! I have just put mechanisms in place where I use better judgment in how I engage and interact with those who I allow into my personal space.

Whole
Sistaz Sharing Stories of Healing and Transformation

www.ingramcontent.com/pod-product-compliance
Lightning Source LLC
Chambersburg PA
CBHW051703090426
42736CB00013B/2521